Trust Your Feelings

Barbara

T.M.

c.a.r.e. Productions Association

Everyone has a body.

Everyone has feelings.

Bodies and feelings go together.

Your feelings come from inside your body.
Everything you see, hear, smell and taste
gives you a feeling.
So does everything you touch.

We all like to touch other people and be touched by them.

Every touch gives you a different feeling.

Usually you want to be touched.
But sometimes you don't.

Some touches feel better than others.

When someone touches you, you may feel happy, safe, comforted. Or you may feel hurt, scared, angry.

What other feelings do you get from touching?

Some touches almost always leave you with
a good feeling.

An arm around your shoulder.
A warm hug.

Holding hands.
A gentle pat on the back.

These touches make you happy. You sense that the person touching you cares about you.

Trust your feelings.

In the same way, people you touch know when you give them caring touches.

What other touches do you like?

Some touching hurts. You can probably think
of lots of hurting touches.

Hitting, kicking, scratching and biting are ones
we all know about. When someone pulls your hair
or bends your arm behind your back it usually
hurts.

Can you think of other touches that hurt?

Sometimes touching starts out feeling good
but ends up hurting.

Like wrestling. Wrestling can be fun when your partner cares about you and is careful not to hurt you. But wrestling can go too far. It can leave you feeling frightened or angry — as though you've had a fight.

Good touching can change to touching that makes you unhappy.

Tickling may make you laugh. You may like it.

But sometimes tickling goes on and on and you end up feeling angry.

Some people don't like being tickled at all.

Different people like different kinds of touching.

Snuggling and cuddling are pleasing touches. You like to be close to someone. Most people like snuggling and cuddling.

But sometimes it's nice to be alone, to stop touching.

You know when you've had enough touching.

Trust your feelings.

There are also touches that may confuse or upset you.

You might feel this way if an adult or teenager touches the private parts of your body.

The private parts of your body are the parts covered by your bathing suit.

Your body is your own.

Your private parts are your own.

A person should not touch your private parts
unless he or she has a good reason to.

Your Mom or Dad may touch them to be sure you are
staying clean and healthy. A nurse or doctor
may examine them to find out if something is
wrong with you.

Your feelings tell you that these touches are O.K.
You sense that the person touching you cares
about you.

But an adult or teenager may want to touch
your private parts without a good reason.
Or a person may want you to touch his or her
private parts.

This person might be someone you know well.
A member of your family. A relative. A neighbour.
An older friend.

Or it might be someone you've never seen before.

Your feelings will probably tell you this is not good caring touching.

Trust your feelings.

An adult or teenager should not touch your private parts without a good reason. This kind of touching is wrong.

If someone tries to touch you in this way, say "no".

You can also say things like:

"I don't like that."

"I'm not allowed to do that."

"I'll tell someone."

Someone may try to talk you into this kind of touching. Someone might even try to trick you or force you into touching that is wrong.

Remember that your body belongs to you. You can say "no".

Tell someone you know and trust about what has happened.

There are people in your family who care and want to help you.

There are people in your community who care
and want to help you.

Most touching is good. It helps you stay happy and healthy.

Touching is one way people tell other people they like them and care about them.

Your body is your own.

Take good care of your body.

Trust your feelings.

c.a.r.e. CARES

Child Abuse Research & Education (**c.a.r.e.**) Productions Association of British Columbia, Canada is a non-profit organization dedicated to the prevention of child sexual abuse. Working with corporate, foundation and public donations as well as government grants, **c.a.r.e.** has concentrated its efforts on gathering and distributing information about the prevention of child sexual abuse.

c.a.r.e.'s major production to date is an educational kit designed for use by a trained leader in schools, or with church and parent groups. This kit is suitable for use with 5 to 9 year old children. It has been endorsed by teachers and parents and is being used in the United States and Canada.

c.a.r.e. was formed in 1980 in Surrey, B.C. by a group of concerned parents and educators. The local police (R.C.M.P.) had approached the Surrey School Board for help in dealing with the problem of child sexual abuse, and the community responded by forming **c.a.r.e.**

ACKNOWLEDGEMENTS

The Board of **c.a.r.e.** Productions Association wishes to acknowledge:

- The society members and its advisors for their volunteer time, professional expertise and continuing guidance.

- The staff of the society, whose creative work and energies helped to develop the publications.

FOR MORE INFORMATION PLEASE WRITE:

CANADA

c.a.r.e. Productions
P.O. Box 183
Surrey, B.C.
V3T 4W8
or telephone (604) 581–5116

AUSTRALIA

c.a.r.e. Productions
36 Ophir Street
Orient Point via
Nowra, N.S.W.
2540
or telephone 473 080

UNITED STATES

c.a.r.e. Productions
Box L #8 - 12th Street
Blaine, WA
98230
or telephone (604) 581–5116